My Pocket Guide

Ohio

By Carole Marsh

THE OHIO EXPERIENCE

Correlates with the Ohio MODEL Competency-Based Social Studies Program

The GALLOPADE GANG

Carole Marsh
Bob Longmeyer
Michele Yother
Michael Marsh
Sherry Moss
Chad Beard
Sue Gentzke
Cecil Anderson

Steven Saint-Laurent
Deborah Sims
Andrew Brim
Andrea Detro
John Raines
Karin Petersen
Billie Walburn
Doug Boston

Kim Holst
Jennifer McGann
Ellen Miller
William Nesbitt, Jr.
Kathy Zimmer
Wanda Coats

Published by
GALLOPADE INTERNATIONAL

www.ohioexperience.com
800-536-2GET • www.gallopade.com

Gallopade is proud to be a member of these educational organizations and associations:

NSSEA

SHOPA MEMBER
School, Home, & Office Products Association

Other Ohio Experience Products

- The Ohio Experience!
- The BIG Ohio Reproducible Activity Book
- The Out-of-This-World Coloring Book
- My First Book About Ohio!
- Ohio "Jography": A Fun Run Through Our Stat
- Ohio Jeopardy!: Answers and Questions About Our State
- The Ohio Experience! Sticker Pack
- The Ohio Experience! Poster/Map
- Discover Ohio CD-ROM
- Ohio "Geo" Bingo Game
- Ohio "Histo" Bingo Game

A Word From the Author... (okay, a few words)...

Hi!
  Here's your own handy pocket guide about the great state of Ohio! It really will fit in a pocket—I tested it. And it really will be useful when you want to know a fact you forgot, to bone up for a test, or when your teacher says, "I wonder . . ." and you have the answer—instantly! Wow, I'm impressed!

Get smart, have fun!
  Carole Marsh

Ohio Basics explores your state's symbols and their special meanings!

Ohio Geography digs up the what's where in your state!

Ohio History is like traveling through time to some of your state's great moments!

Ohio People introduces you to famous personalities and your next-door neighbors!

Ohio Places shows you where you might enjoy your next family vacation!

Ohio Nature - no preservatives here, just what Mother Nature gave to Ohio!

All the real fun stuff that we just HAD to save for its own section!

Ohio Basics

Ohio Geography

Ohio History

Ohio People

Ohio Places

Ohio Nature

Ohio Miscellany

Who Named You?

Ohio's official state name is...

State
Name

Ohio

Word Definition

OFFICIAL: appointed, authorized, or approved by a government or organization

Ohio is one of the states to be on a year-2002 commemorative quarter! Look for it in cash registers everywhere!

Statehood: March 1, 1803

Ohio was the 17th state to ratify the U.S. Constitution.

Seventeen is my lucky number!

A Name of Great Proportions!

Ohio was named for the Ohio River. The Ohio River got its name from the Iroquois Indians. They called the river *Oheo,* which means "great river," or "something great."

In 1811 the first steamboat traveled down the Ohio River. The boat was called the *New Orleans.*

What's In A Name?

"Ohio" is not the only name by which the state is recognized. Like many other states, Ohio has several nicknames, official or unofficial!

State Nicknames

Buckeye State

Mother of Presidents

Heartland of the Nation

The Birthplace of Aviation

Ohio has lots of trees, and lots of nuts. The nuts of one tree reminded the Indians of the eye of a buck deer. This is why Ohio's official nickname is the **"Buckeye State."**

Wooow! You learn something new everyday!

State Capital:
Columbus
Since 1816

State Capital & Capitol

Did you know that 50% of the population of the entire United States lives within 500 miles of Columbus, Ohio?

Word Definition

CAPITAL: a town or city that is the official seat of government
CAPITOL: the building in which the government officials meet

State Government

Who's in Charge Here?

Ohio has three branches:

```
                    GOVERNMENT
                         |
     ┌───────────────────┼───────────────────┐
LEGISLATIVE          EXECUTIVE            JUDICIAL
```

State Government

The state legislative is called the General Assembly.

TWO HOUSES: the Senate (33 members); House of Representatives (99 members)	A governor, lieutenant governor, secretary of state, attorney general, and state treasurer.	SUPREME COURT: a chief justice, plus six other justices

The number of senators and representatives are determined by population, which is counted in the census every ten years; the numbers above are certain to change as Ohio grows and prospers!

When you are 18, according to Ohio law you can vote. So please do! Your vote counts.

8

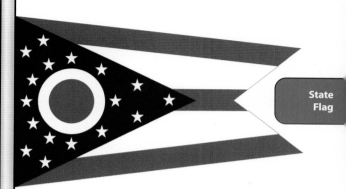

State
Flag

Ohio is the only state in the nation
with a pennant-shaped flag.

As you travel
throughout Ohio,
count the times
you see the Ohio
flag! You might
spot it on
government
vehicles, too!

The State Flag of
Ohio was adopted
in May 1902. It is
always found atop
the state capitol,
and all state,
city and town
buildings.

State Seal

Mount Logan and the rising sun signify that Ohio was the first state west of the Allegheny Mountains.

State Seal & Motto

THE GREAT SEAL OF THE STATE OF OHIO

Word Definition

MOTTO: a sentence, phrase, or word expressing the spirits or purpose of an organization or group

State Motto

With God All Things Are Possible

In the 1860s the Ohio motto was *Imperium in Imperio,* a Latin phrase that means "an empire within an empire."

Adopted in 1959, the state motto was suggested by a 12 year old boy from Cincinnati!

Coccinella Noemnotata is my name!

10

Birds of A Feather

The state bird of Ohio is the Northern Cardinal, *Cardinalis cardinalis,* known for its bright plumage and cheerful song.

State Bird

The male and female Cardinals sing year round; sometimes they even sing together.

BUCKEYE

State
Tree

The Ohio state tree can grow up to 70 feet tall. Although its yellow, white, and red flowers, which bloom in late spring, look beautiful, they give off an awful smell!

SCARLET CARNATION

"For its beauty, its fragrance and its fitness," the red carnation was named the state flower to honor President William McKinley, who was assassinated in 1901. The President, who was from Ohio, wore the flower every day.

State Flower

There are over a hundred varieties of Carnations in colors such as white, yellow, pink, and red. Some have petals with two or three colors!

White Trillium

State Wildflower

The wildflower was used by Indians and early settlers to make medicines, such as astringents, tonics and expectorants.

Just like the state tree, this wildflower is known for its beautiful looks and awful smell.

I don't feel so good...

The Ohio Flint

Indians and early settlers chipped flint to make arrowheads for hunting.

State Stone and Fossil

☐ **To Do List:** Find out what your birthstone is. Can that gem be found in Ohio?

Trilobite

The Trilobite lived millions of years ago. Today we know that Trilobites were marine animals that lived only under the water.

Scientists believe that the Trilobite may be related to the king crabs, scorpions, and spiders that we have today!

A Refreshing Drink

In 1965 **Tomato Juice** became the state beverage of Ohio.

A.W. Livingston, a seed merchant from Reynoldsburg, developed the first edible tomato!

Ohio leads the country in the production of tomato juice, and is second only to California in tomato farming. That's a lot of juice!

Black Racer Snake

State Reptile

The black racer snake is native to all 88 Ohio counties. The snake is sometimes called the "farmer's friend" because it eats rodents like mice that can carry diseases and eat crops. In September or October each year, they go into hibernation until early May.

Black racer snakes only come out during the day. Once the sun sets they hide under a rock or a log.

Beautiful Ohio
by Ballard MacDonald

State Song

Long, long ago, some one I know
Had a little red canoe, in it room for only two
Love found its start, then in my heart
And like a flower grew.

Drifting with the current down a moon-lit stream
While above the heavens in their glory gleam
And the stars on high, twinkle in the sky
Seeming in a paradise of love divine
Dreaming of a pair of eyes that looked in mine.

Beautiful Ohio, in dreams again I see
Visions of what used to be.

Ohio also has an unofficial state rock song. "Hang on Sloopy," was recorded by *The McCoys*, a band from Dayton, and is a favorite of the Ohio State Marching Band.

The Ladybug
— *Coccinella Noemnotata* —

State
Insect

The ladybug is brightly colored to warn its enemies of its nasty taste. Its bad smell also keeps predators away.

During the winter, ladybugs cluster together to keep warm. Sometimes they even get indoors. Have you ever had ladybugs in your house?

White-Tailed Deer

State Animal

In 1988 Governor Richard F. Celeste made the white-tailed deer Ohio's state animal. The bill was requested by a fourth grade class! Do you know how a bill becomes a law?

There are more white-tailed deer in Ohio today than when the settlers first came!

RIDDLE: If the state flower got mixed up with the state animal, what would you have?

Answer: A red deer, or a white-tailed carnation

Our State

Lake Erie

Toledo · Ashtabula ·
Sandusky · Cleveland · Freedom Delightful
Lorain · Oberlin · Kent · Youngstown
Akron
Rubber capital of the world
Lima · Mansfield · Canton
Bolivar
Wapakoneta · Marion · Steubenvil
HIGHEST POINT
Campbell Hill
1,550 ft (472 m)
Above Sea Level
Columbus · Zanesville
OHIO STATE UNIVERSITY
Springfield · Lancaster · Crooked Tree
Dayton · Athens · Marietta
Oxford · Chillicothe
The Village of Indian Hill Ohio's First Capital
Cincinnati ·
Portsmouth
Manchester · Ohio River

Maumee River · Sandusky River · Great Miami River · Scioto River · Ohio River · MARBLEHEAD LIGHTHOUSE · GREAT SERPENT MOUND · ALLEGHENY PLATEAU

Our State

Factories | Tomatoes | Shipping | Soybeans | Corn | Rubber | Tourism | Cattle | Pigs

Ohio used to be much bigger. It was once part of the Northwest Territory which covered what is now Ohio, Illinois, Indiana, Michigan, and Wisconsin!

State Location

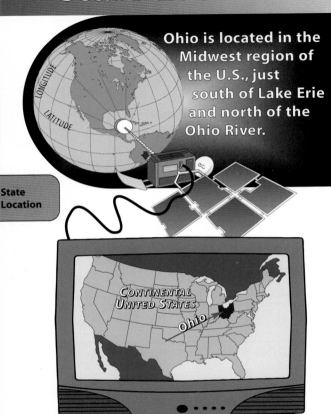

Ohio is located in the Midwest region of the U.S., just south of Lake Erie and north of the Ohio River.

LONGITUDE

LATITUDE

State Location

CONTINENTAL UNITED STATES

Ohio

Word Definition

LATITUDE: Imaginary lines which run horizontally east and west around the globe

LONGITUDE: Imaginary lines which run vertically north and south around the globe

State Neighbors

The banner spells "ON THE BORDER!"

These border Ohio:

States:	Indiana	Michigan
	Kentucky	West Virginia
	Pennsylvania	

| **Bodies of water:** | Lake Erie |
| | Ohio River |

State Neighbors

Michigan

Pennsylvania

Indiana

Ohio

West Virginia

Kentucky

23

You Take the High Road!

East–West
North–South
Area

Ohio is 225 miles (362 kilometers) east to west... or west to east. Either way, it's a long drive!

Total Area: Approx. 44,828 square miles
Land Area: Approx. 40,953 square miles

Ohio is 215 miles (346 km) north to south... or south to north. Either way, it's still a long drive!

Ohio is the 34th largest state!

Highest & Lowest Points

I'll Take The Low Road

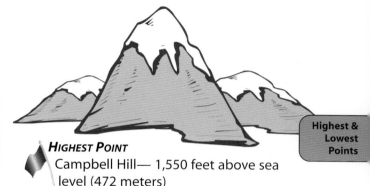

HIGHEST POINT
Campbell Hill— 1,550 feet above sea level (472 meters)

Thousands of years ago glaciers covered Ohio. They cut valleys, rounded hills, and created lakes before they melted away.

LOWEST POINT
Where the Ohio and Miami Rivers meet is only 433 feet (132 meters) above sea level.

I'm Countying on You!

Ohio is divided into 88 counties.

Word Definition

COUNTY: an administrative subdivision of a state or territory

State Counties

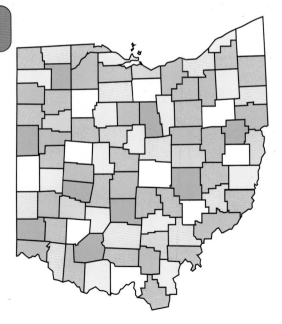

Natural Resources

Forests make up about 25% of Ohio's land area

Word Definition

NATURAL RESOURCES: things that exist in or are formed by nature

Natural Resources

Minerals:
- Salt
- Clay
- Gypsum
- Limestone
- Sandstone
- Sand
- Gravel

Other Resources
- Iron
- Coal
- Petroleum
- Oil
- Natural Gas

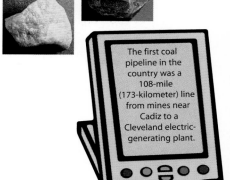

The first coal pipeline in the country was a 108-mile (173-kilometer) line from mines near Cadiz to a Cleveland electric-generating plant.

Weather, Or Not?!

Ohio's climate is temperate but the weather can change quickly. The south experiences milder winters and warmer summers than the north. The rainfall is heavier in the south.

Weather

Highest temperature: 113°F (45°C), Thurman, July 4, 1897

°F=Degrees Fahrenheit °C=Degrees Celsius

Lowest temperature: -39°F (-39°C), Milligan, February 10, 1899

What is heat lightning?

It's just a term we use to describe lightning that is so far away that we can't hear its thunder.

Topography

BACK ON TOP

Ohio's topography includes three land areas:
EAST: Allegheny Plateau
NORTH: Great Lakes Plain
WEST: Till Plains

Ohio falls in two major U.S. topographic regions. Western Ohio falls in the **Central Lowland** region. Eastern Ohio is part of the **Appalachian Highlands.**

> **Word Definition**
> TOPOGRAPHY: the detailed mapping of the features of a small area or district

Only 10% of the 2,500 lakes in Ohio are natural; the others are all man made. Why do we "make" lakes?

Topography

Sea Level
100 m / 328 ft
200 m / 656 ft
500 m / 1,640 ft
1,000 m / 3,281 ft
2,000 m / 6,562 ft
5,000 m / 16,404 ft

29

Rocky Top!

Mountain Range

- Allegheny

Indian Mounds

- Miamisburg Mound
- Mound City
- Serpent Mound

State Geography

Crystal Cave, near Put-in-Bay, is home to one of the world's largest geodes. The single geode is large enough to hold thirty people!

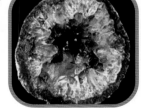

Golly gee! A geode!

Geode: a rock, usually round, having a cavity lined with crystals.

Down the River

Ohio has approximately 40,000 miles of rivers and streams.

The Ohio River winds for 450 miles (724 kilometers) along the Ohio border.

Major Rivers

- **Ohio**
- **Cuyahoga**
- **Maumee**
- **Sandusky**
- **Miami**
- **Scioto**
- **Grand**

The bottom of the Ohio River has been dredged and deepened so that all parts of the river are at least 9 feet (3 meters) deep. This is so the ships can get through without running aground.

Gone Fishin'

Major Lakes & Reservoirs

Lake Erie is one of five lakes that make up the Great Lakes. They were carved by huge glaciers thousands of years ago.

Word Definition

RESERVOIR: a body of water stored for public use

- GRAND LAKE
- LAKE ERIE
- TAPPAN LAKE
- INDIAN LAKE
- MOSQUITO CREEK LAKE
- SENECAVILLE LAKE
- BERLIN LAKE
- PYMATUNING RESERVOIR
- HOOVER RESERVOIR

A TALE OF A FEW CITIES

Have you heard these wonderful Ohio city, town, and crossroad names? Perhaps you can start your own collection!

Cities & Towns

LARGER TOWNS:

Columbus
Cleveland
Cincinnati
Toledo
Akron
Dayton
Canton
Portsmouth
Youngstown
Parma

SMALLER TOWNS:

Coolville
Pleasantville
Frazeysburg
Waldo
Hicksville
Loveland
Irondale
Palestine
Magnetic Springs
Mechanicsburg

Transportation

Major Interstate Highways

I-70, I-71, I-80,
I-90, I-77
U.S. 40, U.S. 23, U.S. 11

The Ohio Turnpike

Railroads

Toledo, Lake Erie, and Western Railroads work to preserve railroad equipment. **Amtrak** provides services throughout the state.

Transportation

Major Airports

Hopkins International
Columbus Airport
Cincinnati Airport
(actually in Covington, Kentucky)

Seaports

St. Lawrence Seaway
Seaplane Anchorage
on Lake Erie and
Ohio River
Cleveland Port Authority

Timeline

- 1669- René-Robert Cavalier, sieur de La Salle, is the first white man to reach what is now Ohio
- 1747- Ohio Company is formed, given land grant on Ohio River
- 1763- France gives up claim on Ohio region to Great Britain
- 1803- Ohio becomes the 17th state
- 1813- American forces defeat British in Battle of Lake Erie
- 1833- Oberlin College, the nation's first coeducational, interracial college, is founded
- 1869- Cincinnati Red Stockings become the nation's first professional baseball team
- 1913- Floods in Ohio kill 430 people
- 1955- The Ohio Turnpike is opened to traffic
- 1959- St. Lawrence Seaway opened
- 1970- Four students killed by National Guard troops at Kent State University during an antiwar demonstration
- 1971- Ohio adopts its first state income tax
- 1985- Western Ohio hit by a tornado that kills 12 people
- 1995- Term limits adopted for governor and other state elected officials
- 2001- Ohio enters the 21st century

The first zoo exhibit without bars, built in 1906, was the monkey island at the Cincinnati zoo. The island is still used today.

35

Here come the humans!

As early as 8000 B.C., Paleo (ancient) people lived in Ohio. They may have originally come across a frozen bridge of land between Asia and today's Alaska. If so, they slowly traveled south and east until some settled in what would one day become the state of Ohio.

Early History

About 2,000 years ago a group of people commonly known as the Mound Builders came to Ohio. They built more than 10,000 mounds in southern Ohio.

Native Americans Once Ruled!

Iroquois Indians lived in Ohio in the 1600s and 1700s. They hunted, fished, and traded goods. They built canoes and used wampum for money. By the 1700s, Ohio had nearly 15,000 people belonging to several different Indian groups. The Eries, Wyandots, Shawnees and Miamis were the largest of these groups.

Early Indians

Word Definition

WAMPUM: beads, pierced and strung used by Indians as money, or for ornaments or ceremonies.

Exploration

Over the rivers and through the woods!

Early explorers came to Ohio in search of fur for trading. English and French traders competed for the land. The English took control of the region in 1763. When the Americans won their independence from Britain in 1783, the colonists began to move across the Allegheny Mountains in search of land. They founded many of the towns that we have today.

Early Explorers

Marietta, the first settlement in Ohio, was named in honor of the French Queen, Marie Antoinette.

I've got his musket balls!

Colonization

Home, Sweet, Home

In 1787, a group of New Englanders called The Ohio Company bought 1.5 million acres (.6 million hectares) of land from Congress. They then posted ads selling the land to other New Englanders.

State Colonies

In April 1788, a riverboat called the *Adventure Gallery,* carried forty-eight men down the Ohio River. The men were delighted by Ohio's rich, dark soil, so they cleared the land and set up a village. The village, called Marietta, was Ohio's first settlement.

In 1800 Chillicothe became the first capital of the "eastern part" of the Northwest Territory, which is now Ohio.

In 1953 researchers discovered that Ohio had never been officially made a state! So President Eisenhower signed a petition making March 1, 1803 Ohio's official date of statehood.

The Daily Grind

In pioneer days, Ohio was an agricultural state. Farms produced corn, wheat, soybeans, tomatoes, and lots of meat. Later, shipbuilding and manufacturing became very important to the economy. Ohio also has oil, natural gas, coal and lots of natural resources for mining.

Key Crop/ Product

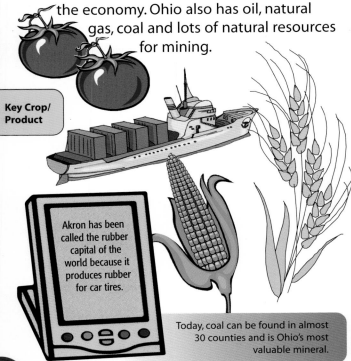

Akron has been called the rubber capital of the world because it produces rubber for car tires.

Today, coal can be found in almost 30 counties and is Ohio's most valuable mineral.

Have You Heard?

- On April 27, 1865, President Lincoln's funeral train rumbled through Ohio. Some people say that on that same day every year they can still hear the train!

- Belaire, Ohio is the site of the "house that Jack built." But Jack, it turns out, is a faithful mule. His owner named the mansion after him and even took the animal on a tour of the house! Jack is now buried beneath an apple tree in the front yard.

Legends & Lore

- "George Washington slept here." Actually, Washington and his men camped in the Ohio River Valley after they heard of a murder down river. The next day they found out that it was an accidental drowning and Washington went on his way.

OF HUMAN BONDAGE

The 1803 Constitution made slavery illegal in Ohio. Many people in Ohio were abolitionists, or people who were against slavery. Since Ohio is very close to other states which had slaves, many runaway slaves fled to Ohio for safety. They traveled from one hiding place to another, along a secret system called the Underground Railroad. Some Ohio abolitionists risked being arrested by helping the runaway slaves. Some farmers would transport slaves under hay in their wagons! The slaves were trying to reach Lake Erie so they could escape to Canada where the slave hunters couldn't catch them.

Slaves and Slavery

Freedom!

In 1776 the thirteen British colonies declared war against Great Britain. They wanted to be able to make their own laws and not pay taxes to a King all the way across the ocean. Ohio wasn't a state yet, but the British wanted to claim this land before the Americans could. However, frontier General George Rogers Clark secured the land for the Americans. The few settlers already in Ohio were nervous as the war waged on. Finally, the colonists defeated the British and won their Independence.

Revolution

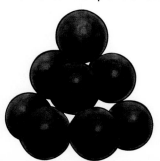

The Society of Cincinnati was an organization of Revolutionary War Officers. Arthur St. Clair named Cincinnati in honor of the society.

Brother

The Civil War was fought between the American states. The argument was over the right of the states to make their own decisions, including whether or not to own slaves. Some of the southern states began to secede (leave) the Union.

The Civil War!

They formed the Confederate States of America. In 1861, some 30,000 Ohioans answered president Lincoln's call for Union troops to fight the Confederate States.

Word Definition

RECONSTRUCTION: the recovery and rebuilding period following the Civil War.

vs. Brother

In the summer of 1863, the war reached Ohio. Confederate General John Hunt Morgan crossed the Ohio River and headed to Cincinnati with 2,000 troops! But Ohio fought back and he was captured in Columbiana County.

The Civil War!

More Americans were killed during the Civil War than during World Wars I and II!

Get It In Writing!

Declaration of Independence, 1776,
Colonists declare war on Great Britain.

Northwest Territory Ordinance,
1787, outlawed slavery, established
guidelines for statehood.

U.S. Constitution, 1787,
Goes into effect 1789

The Treaty of Greenville, 1795,
Indians ceded their Ohio lands to the
United States.

The Ohio Constitution, 1803,
Ohio is officially a state.

Immigrants

WELCOME TO AMERICA!

Ohioans have come to the state from other states and many other countries on almost every continent! As time has gone by, Ohio's population has grown more diverse. This means that people of different races and from different cultures and ethnic backgrounds have moved to Ohio.

State Immigrants

In the past, many immigrants came to Ohio from Germany, Scotland, Ireland, Hungary, Italy, Poland, and other European countries. Many slaves escaped to Ohio during the Civil War. More recently, people have migrated to Ohio from Middle Eastern and Asian countries. Only a certain number of immigrants are allowed to move to America each year. Many of these immigrants eventually become U.S. citizens.

Disasters & Catastrophes!

1900
Flash Floods in Shadyside.

1908
Lake View School in Cleveland catches fire.

1929
Poison gas escapes at a Cleveland clinic.

Farmers have always been fearful of locusts. Swarms of these bugs would come and eat the crops. One swarm was so big it blocked out the sun!

1940
Train wreck in Cuyahoga Falls.

1965
"Palm Sunday" tornadoes.

Legal Stuff

1787

Northwest Territory Ordinance outlawed slavery in the territories.

1836

Congress settles boundary dispute between Ohio and Michigan.

1858

37 men are arrested in the Oberlin-Wellington Rescue of an escaped slave.

1954

The basis for the *Fugitive* movies, Dr. Sam Shepard is accused of killing his wife.

2000

Cincinnati court says that state motto is unconstitutional; goes to appeal.

Women

1852

Harriet Beecher Stowe writes *Uncle Tom's Cabin*, the story of a slave woman's journey to freedom

1872

Victoria Woodhull of Homer becomes the first woman to run for President.

State Women

1920

Women gain suffrage nationally through the 19th Amendment

1922

Florence E. Allen becomes the first U.S. woman to serve as a supreme court justice.

1972

Gloria Steinem, of Toledo, establishes Women's Action Alliance, and *Ms.* magazine.

Word Definition

SUFFRAGE: the right or privilege of voting

Wars

Fight!, Fight!, Fight!

Wars that Ohioans participated in:

- French and Indian War
- Revolutionary War
- War of 1812
- Mexican War
- Civil War
- Spanish-American War
- World War I
- World War II
- Korean War
- Vietnam War
- Persian Gulf War

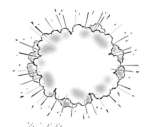

Wars

51

Claim to Fame

"Mother of Presidents"

Warren G. Harding
Twenty-Ninth
U.S. President

Ulysses S. Grant
Eighteenth
U.S. President

Rutherford B. Hayes
Nineteenth
U.S. President

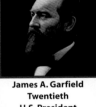

James A. Garfield
Twentieth
U.S. President

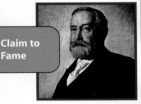

Claim to Fame

Benjamin Harrison
Twenty-Third
U.S. President

William McKinley
Twenty-Fifth
U.S. President

William Howard Taft
Twenty-Seventh
U.S. President

I'm impressed!

It must be something in the water.

52

Indian Tribes

➤➤ Iroquois
➤➤ Eries
➤➤ Delawares
➤➤ Wyandots
➤➤ Shawnees
➤➤ Miami
➤➤ Mississippian

The Hopewell culture built at least 10,000 mounds in Ohio between 100 B.C. and 500 A.D.

Indians in Ohio still hold powwows today!

In 1843 the last of the Indian tribes in Ohio were sent to reservations in Oklahoma and Kansas. Their descendants continue to live there today.

"One small step for man..."

★ ORVILLE AND WILBUR WRIGHT — ★
aviation pioneers from Dayton, invented
the first successful self-propelled plane.
In 1903 they took their first flight.

★ JOHN GLENN — a NASA astronaut
born in Cambridge, became the first
American to orbit the earth in 1962.
In 1998 he returned to space and at
76 years old, became the oldest
person to travel in space.

Aviation Explorers

★ NEIL ARMSTRONG — a NASA
astronaut from Wapakoneta,
became the first man to walk
on the moon, on July 20, 1969.

Neil Armstrong spoke these famous words as
he stepped onto the moon, "One small step
for man, one giant leap for mankind."

State Founders

Founding Fathers

CHRISTOPHER COLUMBUS — Italian explorer who is credited with discovering America in 1492. Columbus, Ohio is named after him!

CÉLERON de BIENVILLE — French explorer; in 1749 planted a series of engraved lead plates along the Ohio river to claim the region for France.

MANASSEH CUTLER and RUFUS PUTNAM — New Englanders who purchased land from the U.S. government and formed The Ohio Company.

ARTHUR ST. CLAIR — The first governor of the Northwest Territory.

MOSES CLEAVELAND — Led a group of surveyors to to the Cuyahoga River and founded Cleaveland (the spelling was later changed).

EDWARD TIFFIN — First governor of Ohio (1803-1807).

Founding Mothers

State Founders

BETSEY MIX COWLES — One of Oberlin College's first graduates.

VICTORIA WOODALL — In 1860, she was the first woman to run for president on the Equal Rights Party ticket.

LUCY WEBB HAYES — She was the first First Lady to earn a college degree. Known as "Lemonade Lucy" because she banned alcohol from the White House.

HELEN HERRON TAFT — First First Lady to be buried at Arlington National Cemetery. She was known for planting hundreds of cherry trees that she received from the Japanese government.

ELIZA BRYANT — Established the Home for Aged Colored People.

CHARLES WADDELL CHESNUT – writer from Cleveland; his short story collections include *The Conjure Woman* and *The Wife of His Youth*.

Awarded the NAACP's Spingarn Medal, 1928.

JESSE OWENS – grew up in Cleveland, ran track at Ohio State, and won 3 gold medals at the 1936 Olympics.

TONI MORRISON – writer from Lorain, best known for her novels including *The Bluest Eye*, *Song of Solomon,* and *Beloved*.

ART TATUM – jazz pianist from Toledo, noted for his solo, as well as trio performances.

CARL STOKES – born in Cleveland; lawyer; politician; and first African-American mayor of a major American city when he was elected mayor of Cleveland in 1967.

Ghosts

DID SOMEONE SAY BOO!?

Many places in Ohio claim to be haunted!
Here are just a few of these ghostly stories...

Beaver Creek Ghost

Buxton Inn's Bonnie Ghost

Sorg Opera House Ghost

Victoria Theater Ghost

The Lady in Gray

Gretchens Lock Ghost

Bowling Green Ghost

Kelton House Ghost

Guests at the Buxton
Inn have reported
being awakened by
a ghostly woman
who just wants
to be sure that
they are enjoying
their stay!

Sports Figures

JOHN HEISMAN – born in Cleveland, he played for Penn State, and was undefeated as Oberlin's head coach in 1892. The Heisman Trophy is named in his honor.

JACK NICKLAUS – born in Columbus, is the all-time leading money winner in golf.

ELI BARNEY OLDFIELD – born in Wauseon, made race car history when he became the first driver to reach the speed of 60 mph (97 km/h) in1903.

PEGGY FLEMING – the 1968 Olympic gold medalist and 1966-68 World Champion, first tried figure skating while she was living in Cleveland.

Sports Figures

CY YOUNG – born in Gilmore, won more games (511) than any other pitcher. The Cy Young award, for the best pitcher in baseball, is named in his honor.

ROGER CLEMENS – born in Dayton, is a five-time Cy Young award winner. This Red Sox pitcher was also the 1986 American League Most Valuable Player.

Entertainers

- ★ BOB HOPE – comedian
- ★ PAUL NEWMAN – actor
- ★ DORIS DAY – actress
- ★ TRACY CHAPMAN – folk singer
- ★ THEDA BARA – silent film actress
- ★ HALLE BERRY – actress

- ★ STEVEN SPIELBERG – film director, *Jaws, Raiders of the Lost Ark, E.T., Schindler's List, Saving Private Ryan,* and other movies
- ★ CLARK GABLE – actor, *Gone With the Wind*
- ★ DWIGHT YOAKAM – country singer
- ★ SARAH JESSICA PARKER – actress
- ★ PHIL DONAHUE – talk show host
- ★ ANNIE OAKLEY – performer with Buffalo Bill's Wild West Show

TRIVIA: Which of the people above is also famous for his line of food products that donates all of its proceeds to charity?

Answer: Paul Newman

PENS ARE MIGHTIER THAN SWORDS!

- ➤ HARRIET BEECHER STOWE – *Uncle Tom's Cabin*
- ➤ ERMA BOMBECK – humorist
- ➤ ROBERT LAWRENCE STINE – children's author, known for his *Goosebumps* and *Fear Street* series.
- ➤ JAMES THURBER – humorist and author, best known for *The Secret Life of Walter Mitty*.
- ➤ LOUIS BROMFIELD – author, Pulitzer Prize Winner, 1926, for *Early Autumn*.
- ➤ O. HENRY (WILLIAM SYDNEY PORTER) – author, (O. HENRY was his nom de plume).

State Authors

- ➤ VIRGINIA HAMILTON – author, *M.C. Higgins the Great*.
- ➤ SHERWOOD ANDERSON – author, *Winesburg, Ohio*.
- ➤ RITA DOVE – poet, youngest and first African-American Poet Laureate of the United States, 1993.

Helen Hooven from Xenia started writing her book, *And the Ladies of the Club*, in the 1920s. She finally finished and published the book in 1986!

nom de plume: French for *pen name*, a fictitious name under which a writer chooses to write

Artists

ELIJAH PIERCE – a barber from Columbus; he whittled in his free time. His shop later became his gallery!

ALICE CHATHAM – sculptor; she created a mask for pilots that fit their heads perfectly. She even designed a mask for the first animal in space, a rhesus monkey.

CATHY LEE GUISEWITE – illustrator; creator of the syndicated "Cathy" comic strip.

ROBERT HENRI – art teacher; founded an art movement focusing on urban life, known as the Ashcan School of Art.

MAYA TING LIN – artist; designed the Vietnam Veterans Memorial in Washington, D.C.

PHILIP CORTELYOU JOHNSON – architect; one of the leaders of the architectural movement known as post-modernism.

TOM WILSON – illustrator; created "Ziggy."

EDUCATORS AND TEACHERS

WILLIAM RAINEY HARPER – born in New Concord, president of Yale, first president of the University of Chicago.

WILLIAM HOLMES MCGUFFEY – President of Cincinnati College and Ohio University. Known for his elementary school readers called *McGuffy's Eclectic Readers*.

ROBERT HENRI – In 1902, this school superintendent wanted his students to have a more hands-on experience, so he founded the 4-H Clubs of America.

DOCTORS AND SCIENTISTS

Educators and Scientists

LILLIAN WALD – nurse from Cincinnati; she pioneered the idea of having nurses in public schools.

THOMAS ALVA EDISON – inventor, best known for the phonograph, had 1,093 patents!

CHARLES FRANKLIN KETTERING – invented the cash register; co-founded the Sloan-Kettering Institute for Cancer Research in New York City.

Military Figures

FAMOUS FIGHTERS

WILLIAM TECUMSEH SHERMAN – born in Lancaster, Civil War Union Army General, known for his "scorched earth policy," earned a reputation for burning down confederate cities in his path.

GEORGE ARMSTRONG CUSTER – Union officer in the Civil War. He fought the Indian tribes, then met his match at the Battle of Little Bighorn.

ULYSSES S. GRANT – commander of the Union forces. He led the Union to victory, and was named General of the Army. Later elected U.S. President.

JOSEPH BRANT – Mohawk leader. He fought on the side of the British in the Revolutionary War.

Military Figures

TECUMSEH – Shawnee Chief; born near Columbus, he sided with the British in the War of 1812 after he lost the 1811 Battle of Tippicanoe.

JOHNNY CLEM – a nine year old boy from Newark, ran away to be a drummer boy in the Union Army.

GOOD GUYS

● DAVE THOMAS – from Columbus, the founder of Wendy's Restaurants, was adopted as a child. He now runs the Dave Thomas Foundation for Adoption.

● JOHNNY APPLESEED – born John Chapman; in the early 1800s he walked across Ohio planting apple orchards.

● JESSE OWENS – from Cleveland, won three gold medals at the 1936 Olympics in Berlin. The leader of Germany, Adolf Hitler, refused to acknowledge Owens because he was black.

BAD GUYS & GIRLS

● CHARLES "PRETTY BOY" FLOYD – robbed banks in northern Ohio. He escaped on his way to jail and robbed even more banks in Oklahoma before the police finally caught up with him.

Good Guys & Bad Guys

● CASSIE CHADWICK – falsely posing as millionaire Andrew Carnegie's daughter, borrowed thousands of dollars from Ohio banks. When her lie was discovered, the banks lost their money and she went to jail.

● JOHN HERBERT DILLINGER – another bank-robber and prison escapee. In 1934 he fooled the FBI by hiring a look-alike to play him. Dillinger escaped and has never been found.

State Leaders and Lawmakers

- Charles Gates Dawes – drew up the Dawes Plan to restore the German economy after World War One.

- Clarence Darrow – lawyer in the famous Scopes trial, where he defended a Tennessee teacher's right to teach the theory of evolution.

- William Green – president of the American Federation of Labor, 1924–52.

- Arthur Schlesinger – assistant to John F. Kennedy, won a Pulitzer Prize for his presidential histories of Andrew Jackson and Kennedy.

- John Sherman – U.S. Representative, 1855–61; U.S. Senator, 1861–77, 1881–97.

- Mary Ellen Withrow – U.S. Treasurer, 1994.

- Robert Alphonso Taft – son of President William Taft; U.S. Senator, 1938–53.

- Frances P. Bolton – U.S. Representative, 1940; first congresswoman to serve as U.N. Delegate, 1953.

- James Middleton Cox – U.S. Representative, 1909–13; Governor of Ohio, 1913–15, 1917–21.

- Salmon Chase – U.S. Senator, 1849–55, 1860; Governor of Ohio, 1855–59; U.S. Secretary of the Treasury 1861–64; Chief Justice of the U.S. Supreme Court, 1864–73.

- William Allen – U.S. Senator, 1843–1849; his statue now stands in the U.S. Capitol.

State Leaders and Lawmakers

Keeping the Faith

Mormon Church in Kirtland – Built in 1833, it was the first Mormon Temple in the U.S.

Monastery of Our Savior – The only Byzantine Catholic monastery in the U.S. is in Steubenville.

Worlds Largest Amish Community – Some 35,000 Amish call Northwest Ohio home.

Hebrew Union College – Established in 1875, it became the first Jewish College to train men to become rabbis.

SCHOOLS

Some of Ohio's colleges and universities:

- ◆ Cleveland State University
- ◆ Kent State University
- ◆ Bowling Green State University
- ◆ Miami University, Oxford
- ◆ Wright State University, Dayton
- ◆ University of Akron
- ◆ Ohio University, Athens
- ◆ The Ohio State University
- ◆ The University of Cincinnati
- ◆ Oberlin College
- ◆ Kenton College
- ◆ Ohio Wesleyan University
- ◆ Antioch College at Yellow Springs
- ◆ Marietta College
- ◆ Case Western Reserve University

Churches and Schools

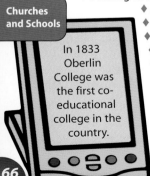
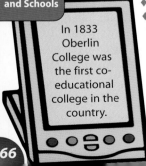

In 1833 Oberlin College was the first co-educational college in the country.

66

HISTORIC SITES

★ Fort Meigs State Memorial
★ McKinley National Memorial
★ Harrison Tomb State Memorial
★ Fort Ancient
★ Columbus State Capitol
★ Fort Recovery
★ Perry's Victory and International Peace Memorial

PARKS

★ Mohican State Park and Forest, just south of Loudonville.

★ Franklin Park Conservatory and Botanical Gardens, in Columbus.

★ Cuyahoga Valley National Recreation Area, between Akron and Cleveland on the Cuyahoga River.

Historic Sites and Parks

★ Serpent Mound State Monument, in northern Adams County. The mounds are believed to be over 2,000 years old.

★ Stonelick State Park, in Pleasant Plain.

Early Residency

★**Lawnfield** – in Mentor, is the home of James A. Garfield, the twentieth U.S. President.

★**Grant's Birthplace State Memorial** – in Point Pleasant; Grant was the eighteenth U.S. President

★ **William Howard Taft National Historic Site** – in Cincinnati; Taft was the twenty-seventh U.S. President.

★ **Warren G. Harding Home and Museum** – in Marion; Harding was the twenty-ninth U.S. President

★**Harrison Tomb State Memorial** – in North Bend; William Henry Harrison was the ninth U.S. President

★**Rutherford B. Hayes Library and Museum State Memorial** – in Fremont; Hayes was the nineteenth U.S. President

A few of Ohio's famous Military Sites

- Pickawillany – French and Indian War battle.
- The Battle of Fallen Timbers, Defiance.
- Salinville – Civil War capture of General John Morgan.
- Firelands – along Lake Erie that was awarded to Connecticut citizens whose farms had been destroyed by the British.
- Virginia Military Tract – along the Ohio River that was awarded to Virginia citizens who had served in the Revolutionary War.

- Refugee Tract – in central Ohio; these lands were awarded to Canadians who had supported the Revolution.
- Western Reserve – around the Cuyahoga River, was set aside for veterans who moved to Ohio.

By the end of the Civil War, some 340,000 Ohioans had served in the Union Forces.

Military Sites

69

Libraries

- FARMER'S LIBRARY – started in Belpre in 1796, was Ohio's first library.
- DAYTON LIBRARY SOCIETY became the first Ohio library incorporated by law in 1805.
- BRUMBACK LIBRARY – in Van Wert, became the first county-wide library in the U.S. in 1901.
- THE HAMILTON COUNTY LIBRARY is the second busiest library system in the country.

Libraries

The Rutherford B. Hayes Presidential Center in Fremont was the first presidential library in the nation, when it opened in 1916.

Zoos & Attractions

COLUMBUS ZOO, Columbus
DAWES ARBORETUM, Newark
METROPARKS ZOO, Cleveland
GREAT LAKES SCIENCE CENTER, Cleveland
CLEVELAND CHILDREN'S MUSEUM, Cleveland
AKRON ZOOLOGICAL PARK, Akron
INVENTURE PLACE, Akron
CEDAR POINT AMUSEMENT PARK, Sandusky
AFRICAN SAFARI WILDLIFE PARK, Port Clinton
TOLEDO ZOO, Toledo
CONEY ISLAND AMUSEMENT PARK, Cincinnati
CINCINNATI ZOO AND BOTANICAL GARDENS, Cincinnati
PARAMOUNT KINGS ISLAND AMUSEMENT PARK, Mason
AMERICANA AMUSEMENT PARK, Middletown
THE DAYTON MUSEUM OF DISCOVERY, Dayton

Zoos & Attractions

LION

Museums

- THE CLEVELAND MUSEUM OF ART, Cleveland
- THE CINCINNATI ART MUSEUM, Cincinnati
- THE TOLEDO MUSEUM OF ART, Toledo
- COLUMBUS MUSEUM OF ART, Columbus
- THE AKRON MUSEUM OF ART, Akron
- THE CINCINNATI MUSEUM OF NATURAL HISTORY, Cincinnati
- THE CLEVELAND MUSEUM OF NATURAL HISTORY, Cleveland
- CLEVELAND MUSEUM OF HEALTH AND HYGIENE, Cleveland
- CENTER OF SCIENCE AND INDUSTRY, Columbus
- WYANDOT POPCORN MUSEUM, Marion
- NEIL ARMSTRONG AIR AND SPACE MUSEUM, Wapakoneta
- WESTERN RESERVE HISTORICAL SOCIETY, Cleveland
- THE U.S. AIR FORCE MUSEUM, Dayton
- TAFT MUSEUM, Cincinnati
- THE BUTLER INSTITUTE OF AMERICAN ART, Youngstown

Museums

- PRO-FOOTBALL HALL OF FAME, Canton
- ROCK AND ROLL HALL OF FAME, Cleveland
- CLEVELAND STYLE POLKA HALL OF FAME

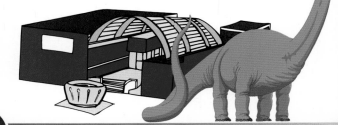

Monuments & Places

MONUMENTS

FORT LAURENS STATE MEMORIAL – near Bolivar, contains the Tomb of the Unknown Patriot of the American Revolution.

MCKINLEY MONUMENT – in Canton, the 100ft (30meter) monument honors our twenty-fifth president.

DON'T GIVE UP THE SHIP

PERRY'S VICTORY AND INTERNATIONAL PEACE MEMORIAL – at Put-In-Bay, in Lake Erie, commemorates General Perry's victory over the British in the War of 1812. He proclaimed, "Don't Give up the Ship!"

SPACE PLACE!

Monuments and Places

NASA's Lewis Research Center – in Cleveland. You can learn about aircraft propulsion, satellites and aerospace technology!

The Arts

OHIO BALLET COMPANY OF AKRON – **Akron**

CLEVELAND SYMPHONY ORCHESTRA – founded in 1918, *TIME Magazine* called them the "best band in the land," in 1994.

CINCINNATI OPERA – this theaterless group performed at the Cincinnati Zoo for 62 years before they moved into Music Hall!

THE CLEVELAND PLAYHOUSE – is one of America's oldest theater companies.

MAY FESTIVAL – in Cincinnati, it is the oldest continuing choral and music festival in the world.

The Arts

Mount Vernon native Daniel Emmett wrote "I Wish I Was in Dixie" while in New York City. The song was later adopted by the Confederacy.

SHORES

Ohio shares the shoreline of Lake Erie with Michigan, Pennsylvania, New York, and Canada.

LIGHTHOUSES

Built in 1821, the Sandusky lighthouse is still standing. Ohio once had as many as ten lighthouses on Lake Erie.

Seashores & Lighthouses

ROADS

THE NATIONAL ROAD – is a land route used by pioneer families crossing Ohio.

MCKINLEY STREET – in Bellefontaine, is only 30 feet long, the shortest street in the world!

BRIDGES, CANALS, AND RAILROADS

ZANESVILLE Y-BRIDGE – splits over the Muskingum River to connect the different sections of the city.

THE OHIO AND ERIE CANAL – built in 1832, ran from Portsmouth on the Ohio River to Cleveland on Lake Erie.

THE MIAMI AND ERIE CANAL – built in 1845, stretched from Cincinnati to Toledo.

THE ERIE AND KALAMAZOO – completed in 1836, was Ohio's first railroad. Pretty soon Ohio was connected to so many major cities that it earned the nickname, "Gateway to the West."

Swamps and Caverns

SWAMPS

THE BLACK SWAMP REGION is in the Northwest along Lake Erie. The moist soil was perfect for farming so the early settlers drained the water and planted crops.

CAVERNS

- OHIO CAVERNS
- SEVEN CAVES
- INDIAN TRAIL CAVERNS
- HOCKING HILLS
- SENECA CAVERNS
- ZANE CAVERNS

A *spelunker* is a person who goes exploring caves!

QUESTION:
- Which is the stalagmite?
- Which is the stalactite?

ANSWER: Stalactites are long, tapering formations hanging from the roof of a cavern, produced by continuous watery deposits containing certain minerals. The mineral-rich water dripping from stalactites often forms conical stalagmites on the floor below.

ANIMALS OF OHIO

Ohio animals include:

Frogs
Shrews
White-tailed Deer
Beavers
Bobcats
Coyotes
Foxes

Moles
Muskrats
Opossums
Rabbits
Salamanders
Skunks
Snakes
Turtles

Animals

The opossum is North America's only marsupial (pouched mammal). An opossum may "play possum" and pretend it is dead to escape an enemy!

Take a Walk on The Wild Side

THE WILDS is a 9,000 acre (3,600 hectare) reserve in Muskingum County. Endangered animals such as Asian Wild Horses, North American Red Wolves, giraffes, and White Rhinoceri roam the hills and valleys. The hope is that the animals born here can be returned to their natural habitat.

PEREGRINE FALCONS have been released off of buildings in major Ohio cities since 1986. The volunteers hope that the birds will establish a nesting pattern and produce chicks.

Ohio has nineteen state parks that cover 177,000 acres of land.

Look! I think I see one!

Wildlife Watch

Birds

YOU MAY SPY THESE BIRDS!

Wood Duck

Blackbirds
Cardinals
Chickadees
Cowbirds
Grosbeaks
Herons
Thrashers
Geese
Wild Turkey
Pheasants
Teals

Quail

Wren

Mourning Dove

Tern

Thrush

A hummingbird's wings beat 75 times a second—so fast that you only see a blur! They make short, squeaky sounds, but do not sing.

Birds

Ruffed Grouse

Insects

Don't let these Ohio bugs bug you!

Beetle
Cicada
Cricket
Dragonfly
Firefly
Honeybee
Katydid
Mayfly
Mosquito
Moth
Termite
Walking Stick
Weevil
Yellow Jacket

Bumblebee

Butterfly

Ants

Ladybug

Praying
Mantis

Grasshopper

Whirligig Beetles
have two pairs of
eyes — one pair
looks above the
water, the other
looks under it!

Fish

SWIMMING IN OHIO WATERS:

Bass
Bluegill
Carp
Catfish
Crappie
Bluegill
Darter
Muskellunge
Perch
Pickerel
Pike
Suckers
Trout
Walleye
Salmon

Fish

Crystal Lake in Portage County is home to the
only freshwater jellyfish in the country!

Lake Erie

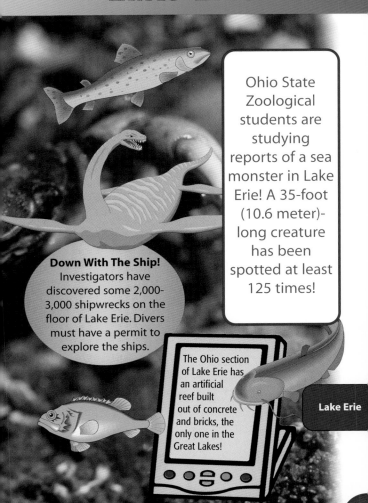

Ohio State Zoological students are studying reports of a sea monster in Lake Erie! A 35-foot (10.6 meter)-long creature has been spotted at least 125 times!

Down With The Ship!
Investigators have discovered some 2,000-3,000 shipwrecks on the floor of Lake Erie. Divers must have a permit to explore the ships.

The Ohio section of Lake Erie has an artificial reef built out of concrete and bricks, the only one in the Great Lakes!

Lake Erie

Amazing
Ohio Discoveries

• The largest skeleton of a giant ground sloth in the world is now housed at the Akron Museum of Natural History.

• In 1926, a Johnstown resident found the remains of a mastodon skeleton while he was working in his garden!

• Today, Ohio has 180 mastodon fossils. The largest and most complete is at the Ohio Historical Center in Columbus.

• In 1990, skeletons of prehistoric elk-moose, giant beavers, wild boar and the short-faced bear were discovered at the Indian Trail Caverns.

Fossils

The word fossil comes from the Latin word *fossilis,* which means "something dug out of the ground."

TREEMENDOUS!

THESE TREES TOWER OVER OHIO:

White Ash
Sycamore
Wild Cherry
Beech
Birch
Buckeye
Butternut
Hemlock
Tulip
Locust
Maple
Oak
Poplar
Elm
Pine

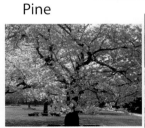

Wildflowers

Are you crazy about these Ohio wildflowers?

Yellow-fringed orchid
Lily
Wild Indigo
Azalea
Blue Sage
White Trillium
Sassafras

A red trillium smells like rotten meat! This attracts flies, which pollinate the plant. The roots of this flower were once used to treat rattlesnake bites.

Cream of the Crops

Ohio's principal agricultural products:

Chickens

Corn

Milk

Tomatoes

Yams
(sweet potatoes)

Beef Cattle

Soybeans

Turkeys

Wheat

Cream of
the Crops

Hogs

Apples

Hay

OHIO RECORDS

JERRI MOCK of Columbus was the first woman to fly solo around the world in 1964.

FIRST PRESIDENTIAL RADIO BROADCAST was delivered by Warren G. Harding in 1922.

THE FIRST KINDERGARTEN was set up in Columbus by German settlers in 1838.

FIRST PROFESSIONAL BASEBALL TEAM – the Cincinnati Red Stockings organized in 1866.

THE FIRST HOTDOG was invented in 1900, by Harry Stevens of Niles.

CHEWING GUM was invented by a Mt. Vernon dentist as a way to clean your teeth between meals.

THE TALLEST ROLLER COASTER is the Millenium Force at Cedar Point in Sandusky. The coaster is 310 feet (1,023 meters) tall, and drops funseekers at an eighty degree angle!

Festivals and Events

TWIN DAYS – held in Twinsburg every August; thousands of twins, triplets and quadruplets attend the event.

FESTIVAL OF LIGHTS – one at the Cincinnati Zoo and one in Fountain Square; held in November and December, Cincinnati sparkles for the Holidays.

SOAP BOX DERBY – held every August in Akron; kids from all over the country come to compete.

DAYTON INTERNATIONAL AIR SHOW – is one of the top air shows in the country. It's fitting that it's held in the hometown of the Wright Brothers.

ANNIE OAKLEY DAYS – every July in Greenville, you can learn more about this sharp shooting gal.

OKTOBERFEST – or German American Day, is held in the German district just south of downtown Columbus.

Festivals

Calendar

Martin Luther King Day, *in January*	Presidents Day, *3rd Monday in February*	Memorial Day, *last Monday in May*
Independence Day, *July 4*	Columbus Day, *2nd Monday in October*	Veteran's Day, *November 11*

Notes:

Settlers in Marietta held a huge celebration for their first Fourth of July in 1788.

Famous Food

Ohio is famous for the following delicious foods...

Cincinnati Chili
Apple Butter
Indian Corn Stew
Scrapple
Sugar Cream Raisin Pie

Biscuits and Gravy
Smoked Ham
Pizza
Sorghum
Hotdogs

...and Food Makers!

HECTOR BOARDI- Chef Boy-ar-dee

JEROME SMUCKER- Smucker's Jelly

BERNARD KROGER- Kroger Grocery Stores

DAVE THOMAS- Founder of Wendy's

BOB EVANS- Bob Evans Farm Sausage

VERNON STOUFFER-
The Stouffer Corporation

FERDINAND SCHUMACHER-
Quaker Oats

Yumm, yumm! Come and get it!

Business & Trade

The state of Ohio produces a wide variety of products for people to use all over the world. Ohio is one of the country's leading manufacturing states. Many important companies got their start here in Ohio.

PROCTOR AND GAMBLE – Cincinnati

GOODYEAR TIRE AND RUBBER – Akron

SHERWIN-WILLIAMS – Cleveland

CHAMPION SPARKPLUG – Toledo

The world's first billionaire, John D. Rockefeller, got his start in Ohio. His company, Standard Oil, once controlled almost 95% of the nation's oil. Rockefeller donated much of his fortune for projects such as the University of Chicago, and Rockefeller Center in New York.

Business and Trade

State Books & Websites

My First Book About Ohio by Carole Marsh
America the Beautiful: Ohio by Sylvia McNair
From Sea to Shining Sea: Ohio by Dennis Fraden
Hello USA: Ohio by Karen Sirvaitis
Let's Discover the States: Ohio by the Aylesworths
Portrait of America: Ohio by Kathleen Thompson
The Ohio Experience by Carole Marsh

COOL OHIO WEBSITES

StateWebsites
http://www.50states.com
http://www.state.oh.us

To learn about Ohio
http://www.ohioexperience.com

Historical Documents
http://www.ohioexperience.com/gallopade/sitepages/
histdoc.html

Travel Guides
http://www.moon.com

Ohio, off the Beaten Path
http://www.globe-pequot.com

Ohio
Glossary

GLOSSARY WORDS

abolitionist: a person opposed to slavery

arboretum: a place for the study and display of trees

colony: a region controlled by a distant country

commonwealth: for the good of the people

constitution: a document outlining the role of a government

endangered: in danger of becoming extinct

emancipation: to be set free

immigrant: a person who comes to a new country to live

population: the total number of people living in an area

revolution: the overthrow of a government

scrapple: a fried mixture of pork scraps, meal, and seasonings

secede: to voluntarily give up being a part of an organized group

sorghum: syrup made from plant juices

Ohio
Spelling Bee

Here are some special Ohio-related words to learn! To take the Spelling Bee, have someone call out the words and you spell them aloud or write them on a piece of paper.

SPELLING WORDS

Allegheny	Kalamazoo
Ashtabula	Marietta
Bellefontaine	Maumee
Buckeye	Mosquito
Carnation	Oberlin
Cincinnati	Put-in-Bay
Cleveland	Sandusky
Columbus	Steubenville
Cuyahoga	Tecumseh
Fort Pickawillany	Toledo
glaciers	Tuscarawas
Hocking	Wyandots
Iroquois	Xenia

Spelling List

ABOUT THE AUTHOR...

CAROLE MARSH has been writing about Ohio for more than 20 years. She is the author of the popular Ohio State Stuff series for young readers and creator, along with her son, Michael Marsh, of "Ohio Facts and Factivities," a CD-ROM widely used in Ohio schools. The author of more than 100 Ohio books and other supplementary educational materials on the state, Marsh is currently working on a new collection of Ohio materials for young people. Marsh correlates her Ohio materials to Ohio's Model Competency Based Program. Many of her books and other materials have been inspired by or requested by Ohio teachers and librarians.

About the Author

Editorial Assistant/Student Intern:
Jennifer McGann